Sacred Animals

KRIS WALDHERR

Sacred Animals

HARPERCOLLINSPUBLISHERS

For Melanie S. Donovan,
editor and friend,
with affection and gratitude

Sacred Animals
Copyright © 2001 by Kris Waldherr
Printed in Hong Kong. All rights reserved.
www.harperchildrens.com

Library of Congress Cataloging-in-Publication Data
Waldherr, Kris.   Sacred animals / by Kris Waldherr.
    p.   cm.
    ISBN 0-688-16379-3 — ISBN 0-688-16380-7 (lib. bdg.)
    1. Animals—Religious aspects—Juvenile literature.   2. Animals—
Mythology—Juvenile literature.   [1. Animals—Religious aspects.
2. Animals—Mythology.]   I. Title.
BL439.W35   2001   00-049877
291.2'12—dc21

Typography by Carla Weise
1 2 3 4 5 6 7 8 9 10
❖
First Edition

S*acred Animals* was created out of my love and respect for animals everywhere. It is intended as a celebration of their many shapes and sizes, strengths and talents, as revealed in mythology and folklore from around the world. In an earlier book, *The Book of Goddesses*, I explored the powers and beauties of women as described in goddess myths. In *Sacred Animals* I've sought to do the same for the animal kingdom.

The rich diversity of animals and their myths remind us of nature's generosity of form and function. As I worked on this book, I encountered this bounty at every turn, especially as I began the process of deciding which animals to feature within these pages. How could I choose to include cat but not dog? Or invite fox over wolf? In the delicately balanced ecosystems that make up our world, no one animal is more important than another. I have tried to reflect this natural balance in the sampling of animals and myths included here.

This book is organized into four sections representing the four elements: earth, air, water, and fire. Four animals are included in each section, each associated with a particular element in folklore around the world. Though there is a wonderful variety among these myths, it is amazing how many aspects of animal legends resonate with one another, even though the cultures that created them may be vastly different and thousands of miles apart. As you enter the world of *Sacred Animals*, I hope that these sacred stories will speak to you as they have to other insightful people since the beginning of time.

Earth

Cat

Fox

Snake

Bear

Air

Raven

Dove

Butterfly

Bat

Water

Dolphin

Carp

Seal

Frog

Fire

Falcon

Dragon

Chimera

Phoenix

EARTH

Cat

Fox

Snake

Bear

Cat

Valued for their hunting skills as well as their beauty, cats have been honored throughout time for their apparently mysterious, even magical, powers. Their glowing eyes can see through the darkest night, and their quick claws have kept barns free of rats, mice, and snakes for centuries. Perhaps because of cats' ability to escape from dangerous situations, some people even claim they have nine lives.

Legends tell of the cat's supernatural powers. The ancient Greeks associated the cat with the moon goddess, Artemis, also renowned as a hunter. In Europe cats were said to become invisible at will and to be the favorite familiar of witches and wizards. On the sea, sailors used cats to predict bad weather because they react strongly to changes in barometric pressure. They also kept them onboard to hunt down that inevitable stowaway, the rat. Some feared that a displeased cat could stir up a tempest with the flick of the tail. On land, many avoided black cats, believing that they brought bad luck to any who crossed their paths. But in Japan and China, cats were honored as good-luck talismans and kept inside the home.

Cats and people have lived together for thousands of years. Only dogs have had as long and as close a relationship with us. While cats are prized pets all over the globe, no culture has ever surpassed the ancient Egyptians in appreciating their grace and usefulness.

Four thousand years ago, the cat was worshiped in cities along the Nile River as the sacred animal of Bastet, the Egyptian goddess of happiness, love, pregnancy, and childbirth. Surviving statues and pictures show the goddess, with the head of a cat, holding an ankh, a symbol of fertility and eternal life. Records from the time of the pharaohs tell us that Bastet's temples were home to hundreds of cats and kittens, which were cared for with loving devotion by her followers. Some Egyptians revered their cats so much that they would shave their eyebrows as a sign of grief when their pet died. Mummified cats have also been found in pharaohs' tombs, placed there to help guide their royal masters to the afterlife.

Fox

The fox is a crafty animal in both myth and life. Fleet of foot and quick of wit, he is renowned as a master thief of hens and other small animals raised for the dinner table. No matter what precautions the farmer takes, the clever fox seems able to get around them. Indeed, to "outfox" somebody means to outsmart him or her. This elusive creature is both the hunter and the hunted, a symbol of rebellion and of beating the odds. Many Native American tribes depict the fox as a cunning trickster and thief in their myths. In Scandinavia the northern lights, or aurora borealis, is called "the light of the fox" because the unearthly shifting colors in the sky mislead and trick the eye. Many Chinese thought white foxes were helpful spirits and black foxes were malevolent ones. Sometimes a fox spirit would shape-shift into a beautiful woman, the better to woo a man to her will for good or evil.

But more positively, the fox is also associated with wealth gained through creative problem solving. In many cultures, this animal is revered as an omen of successful farming. Among the Dogon of Mali, a country in Africa, a powerful god called Pale Fox first brought the gift of grain to the people and saw that it was distributed throughout the land. Inari, a Japanese god of food and rice worshiped to this day, sometimes takes on the form of a fox to visit mortals. There are over forty thousand shrines dedicated to the powerful deity along the twisted mountain paths of Japan's highlands. These shrines, often guarded by majestic red Torii gates, contain statues that depict the god flanked by two foxes. Harvest festivals devoted to a female incarnation of Inari take place at the autumnal equinox in late September. Rice cakes filled with red bean paste, raw rice, and sake (a sweet rice wine), are offered at the fox god's shrines in thanks for a bountiful harvest.

Snake

No other animal has conjured up more contradictory emotions and myths around the world than the snake. It is a symbol of creation and of destruction, of wisdom and of deceit. In Greco-Roman mythology the snake was sacred to Asclepius, the god of medicine. Artists often depicted the god carrying a staff with two snakes twined around it as an emblem of the power to heal. Called a caduceus, this symbol is still used by doctors today. The ouroboros, another universal symbol with Greek origins, is a serpent forming a perfect ring by holding its tail in its mouth. It stands for the eternal circle of life.

The snake is often associated with creation stories. According to Judeo-Christian tradition, a serpent convinced the first woman, Eve, to share fruit from the tree of knowledge with the first man, Adam, with whom she lived blissfully in the Garden of Eden. Since eating this fruit was against God's commandment, a heavy price was exacted: God banished Adam and Eve from paradise and decreed that snake and humankind must spurn each other forever. In contrast to the story of Adam and Eve, Northwest Australian Aborigines believe that the great rainbow serpent, Kalseru, created all life. And a North African creation myth tells how the creator first made a cosmic snake and then divided it into seven parts to make up the world.

In Norse mythology snakes represented the elemental forces of chaos held in check by the firm rule of their gods and goddesses. One such snake was Jormungand, the World Serpent. This monstrous offspring of Loki, the mischievous fire god, and the giantess Angrboda was confined by the gods to the depths of the ocean, where he coiled around the earth, biting his tail and biding his time. The Norse also believed that evil serpents sought to undermine Yggdrasil, the mighty ash tree that held the entire cosmos in its roots. The most powerful of these was Nidhogg, a huge snake that gnawed perpetually at Yggdrasil's deepest root, striving in vain to topple the World Tree.

Bear

Bears and people have much in common. For centuries we competed for the same foods and the same territory. The bear is also one of the few animals whose skeletal structure enables it to walk upright like a human. Not surprisingly, many cultures considered the bear to be the animal most like us. There are countless stories of humans turning into bears. One Greco-Roman myth relates how the jealous queen of the gods, Hera, shape-shifted the nymph Callisto into a bear after she bore a son to Zeus, Hera's husband. The boy, Arcas, grew up to be a great hunter. When Arcas inadvertently pursued the bear that had been Callisto, Zeus prevented the boy from killing his mother by pulling mother and son into the sky and transforming them into constellations. These two constellations are known today as Ursa Major—Great Bear—and Ursa Minor—Little Bear. In the east a Chinese myth claims that Da Yu, the mythical founder of the Xia Dynasty, changed himself into a bear after a great flood in order to dig passes through the mountains and create the mighty rivers that connect China.

Norse sagas tell of a group of fearsome warriors who fought with such strength and ferocity, it was whispered that they actually turned into bears in battle. The bearskin shirts worn by these Viking raiders earned them the name of "berserks." Centuries after they faded into legend, "to go berserk" still means to rage like a savage beast.

According to Navaho tradition, all living things are interconnected, but the bond between bear and human is a special one. The Navaho will not hunt bears as food, for to eat a bear would be as offensive as to eat a brother. It is also believed that the bear is one of the Mountain People, powerful guardian spirits who govern the forces of nature. If a person injures or kills a bear, even in self-defense, he can be afflicted with bear sickness. This terrible illness affects the sufferer's mind and body and can only be cured by performing a series of ceremonies called the Mountain Way.

AIR.

Raven

Dove

Butterfly

Bat

Raven

With its striking black plumage, impressive wingspan, and loud, hoarse call, the raven cannot help but draw attention to itself. In many mythologies this bird is viewed as a supernatural messenger or guide. The ancient Norse associated the raven with Odin, the ruler of the gods. Every day Odin sent two ravens, Hugin (Thought) and Munin (Memory) to fly about the earth as his spies. When they returned, the birds would sit on the god's shoulders and whisper to him all they had seen and heard. The raven is a messenger in the Bible, too. After God flooded the world, a raven was sent from Noah's ark to search for land.

Yet many cultures see the raven as an ominous symbol of death and misfortune. The Celtic war goddess, Morrigan, was believed to circle over battlefields in the form of a raven, swooping down to drink the blood of the dying. In Yorkshire, England, children were told that the Great Black Bird would carry them away if they were bad. Ironically, the raven also stands as a good-luck charm for the English. A flock of ravens has lived for centuries in the Tower of London. An old superstition says the British Empire will never fall as long as these ravens remain in the Tower. Just to be on the safe side, the birds' wings are clipped so that they cannot fly away.

Native American peoples of the Pacific Northwest think of the raven in a different way. To them Raven is the creator spirit as well as a mischievous trickster. One legend tells that Raven created the earth but had to trick a powerful sky chief to bring light to this world. This chief treasured two things: his cedar box, which contained the moon and the sun, and his beautiful daughter. Clever Raven arranged to be reborn as the daughter's baby, knowing the chief wouldn't be able to resist his own grandson. Baby Raven cried and cried to play with the precious box until the sky chief finally gave in. Immediately Raven returned to his bird form and flew away laughing, holding the box of light tight in his talons.

Dove

The dove, so ethereal in its beauty, represents the hopes all humans hold for love, peace, and union with the divine. In many cultures, the white dove was sacred to love goddesses, including Aphrodite in Greece, Venus in Rome, and Ishtar in Mesopotamia. Even today white doves are often released after wedding ceremonies to represent the newlyweds' commitment to each other. One old English folktale says that if two doves fly off together, the marriage will be a happy one, but if the doves separate, the couple is destined to part.

In the Vedic religion of India, the dove is associated with Yama, a god who ruled over the worthy dead in a realm of light and happiness. Gypsies, the traveling people of Europe, also relate the dove with the otherworld of the afterlife. They believe that female ancestors sometimes take the form of a dove to communicate with the living. Christians revere it as a symbol of the divine, believing the dove represents the holy spirit, or the aspect of God in all living things. Their sacred art often depicts saints with a luminous white dove hovering over their heads, signifying their divine inspiration.

Throughout the Western Hemisphere, the most widely known dove story comes from the Bible. According to the Book of Genesis, God was angered by people's wrongdoing and caused torrential rains to flood the Earth. But before the deluge began, God warned his prophet, Noah, who took his family and two of each creature aboard a great ark. When the rains finally stopped, Noah sent out a raven to fly over the water and find land. When it never came back, Noah sent a dove, which returned to the ark exhausted. Again Noah sent out the dove, and this time it arrived with an olive leaf in its beak. But the third time, the dove did not return, confirming that dry land had reappeared at last. A dove holding an olive branch in its beak is a Judeo-Christian symbol of peace, commemorating the promise God made after the Flood that he would never again vent his anger at humans on the natural world.

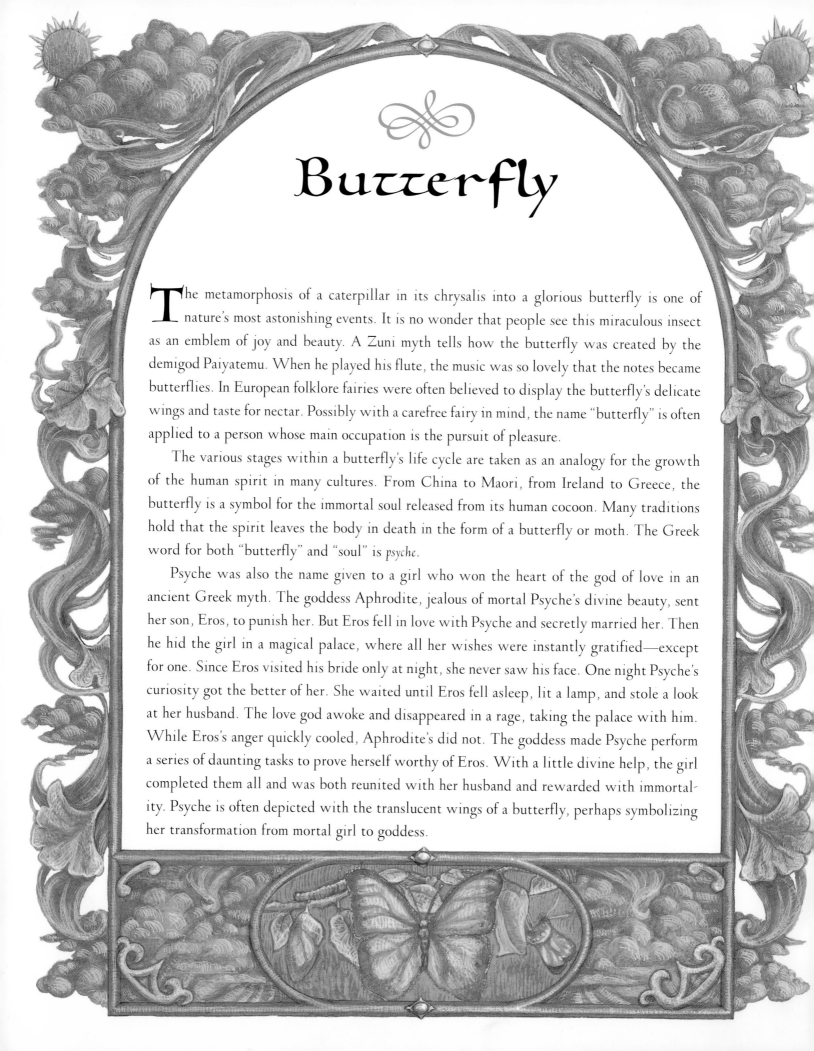

Butterfly

The metamorphosis of a caterpillar in its chrysalis into a glorious butterfly is one of nature's most astonishing events. It is no wonder that people see this miraculous insect as an emblem of joy and beauty. A Zuni myth tells how the butterfly was created by the demigod Paiyatemu. When he played his flute, the music was so lovely that the notes became butterflies. In European folklore fairies were often believed to display the butterfly's delicate wings and taste for nectar. Possibly with a carefree fairy in mind, the name "butterfly" is often applied to a person whose main occupation is the pursuit of pleasure.

The various stages within a butterfly's life cycle are taken as an analogy for the growth of the human spirit in many cultures. From China to Maori, from Ireland to Greece, the butterfly is a symbol for the immortal soul released from its human cocoon. Many traditions hold that the spirit leaves the body in death in the form of a butterfly or moth. The Greek word for both "butterfly" and "soul" is *psyche*.

Psyche was also the name given to a girl who won the heart of the god of love in an ancient Greek myth. The goddess Aphrodite, jealous of mortal Psyche's divine beauty, sent her son, Eros, to punish her. But Eros fell in love with Psyche and secretly married her. Then he hid the girl in a magical palace, where all her wishes were instantly gratified—except for one. Since Eros visited his bride only at night, she never saw his face. One night Psyche's curiosity got the better of her. She waited until Eros fell asleep, lit a lamp, and stole a look at her husband. The love god awoke and disappeared in a rage, taking the palace with him. While Eros's anger quickly cooled, Aphrodite's did not. The goddess made Psyche perform a series of daunting tasks to prove herself worthy of Eros. With a little divine help, the girl completed them all and was both reunited with her husband and rewarded with immortality. Psyche is often depicted with the translucent wings of a butterfly, perhaps symbolizing her transformation from mortal girl to goddess.

Bat

Fueled by centuries of superstition, misconceptions abound about the bat. In reality this shy, intelligent animal often helps humans by eating mosquitoes and other insects that carry disease. Still, folk traditions associate the bat with the powers of darkness, perhaps fueled by its nocturnal life and the unusual eating habits of one species found only in Central and South America.

The vampire bat feeds by biting animals with two sharp fangs and lapping blood from the wound. This small bat rarely harms its victims and prefers cattle to humans, yet the vampire associated with this species has become a universal symbol of supernatural evil.

Tales of the vampire, or nosferatu, were spread throughout Europe by Gypsies, who warned of an undead monster that abandoned its coffin between sunset and sunrise to prey on the unwary. This sinister creature glided unseen through the night disguised as a bat, a tendril of mist, or a wolf as it sought to satisfy its appetite for human blood. Those unfortunates who died from the vampire's bite were doomed to join the ranks of the undead themselves. This Eastern European folktale was popularized by the nineteenth-century novel *Dracula* by the Irish author Bram Stoker. Count Dracula, with his eerie castle in Transylvania, hypnotic gaze, and ability to transform himself into a huge black bat, has since become a legend in his own right.

Luckily the gentle bat is better appreciated in Asia, where it is seen as a omen of good luck. The Chinese character "fu" stands for both bat and happiness, and Fu-xing, the Taoist god of happiness, is symbolized by a bat. A pair of bats is associated with Shou-xing, the god of long life, and five bats are thought to represent the five blessings of health, wealth, long life, peace, and happiness.

WATER

Dolphin

Carp

Seal

Frog

Dolphin

Perhaps because these intelligent marine mammals seem to be equally interested in us, people are fascinated by dolphins. Maritime cultures around the world tell stories of friendly dolphins saving sailors' lives. One amazing true story about a boy and a wild dolphin who shared a special bond was recorded by the Roman naturalist Pliny the Elder in 70 C.E. Each day the dolphin would meet the boy at the shore to carry him on its back across a bay to school and then bring him home again after class. When the boy suddenly died, the dolphin missed his human friend so much that it died, too, from sorrow.

The dolphin appears as a guide and helper in many Greek myths. Delphi, the spiritual center of the ancient Greek world, derived its name from the Greek word for "dolphin," *delphinos,* because the god Apollo was believed to have led his priests to that sacred shrine in the form of a dolphin. Another legend tells how the sea god Poseidon fell in love with the nymph Amphitrite. He asked her to be his wife, but she wasn't sure she wanted to marry him and hid herself deep in the Atlantic Ocean. A dolphin found the shy nymph and brought her to Poseidon, who finally convinced Amphitrite to reign beside him as queen of the sea. The sea god rewarded the loyal dolphin by elevating it to the heavens as a constellation.

The dolphin is also associated with the afterlife. Ancient rock paintings of the Australian Aborigines depict dolphins aiding fishermen by herding fish into their nets. It was believed these dolphins were souls of the dead, returned to watch over their people.

But perhaps the loveliest dolphin legend comes from the Chumash people of California. In this story the grandmother goddess built a rainbow bridge so that the Chumash could cross the Pacific Ocean from Siberia to the New World. She warned the people that if they looked down at the water, they would fall in and drown. Some did not heed the goddess's warning, but the grandmother could not bear to let her children die. Instead she transformed them into beautiful dolphins.

Carp

(GOLDFISH)

The carp is believed to be the first fish ever kept by humans. Records show that the Chinese bred it for food as early as 1000 B.C.E. Carp is still enjoyed today in Asia and Eastern Europe. Jewish cooks choose it for making gefilte fish, the savory fish balls traditionally served at Passover seders and at Rosh Hashanah, the Jewish New Year. But it is their ornamental rather than their edible qualities that have most endeared carp to us.

For thousand of years, koi carp, commonly called goldfish, have enchanted people with their golden scales and gossamer fins. Chinese monks are credited with domesticating goldfish. Now these elegant creatures grace garden ponds and aquariums around the globe.

They are regarded as luck charms in many cultures. In Japan special carp-shaped streamers, called *koinobori*, are flown every May fifth. Traditionally this Japanese festival, called *Tango no Sekku*, was a day for families to celebrate sons. Since 1948, May fifth has honored both boys and girls and is now a Japanese national holiday called Children's Day.

Throughout Asia the carp is also seen as a favorite shape-shifting spirit. A goldfish even plays the fairy godmother role in a Chinese Cinderella story. In this fairy tale a poor orphan girl named Yeh-Shen had only one friend, a carp with unusual gold eyes. But the girl's cruel stepmother killed the fish and served it for supper. That night the carp's spirit came to Yeh-Shen, instructing her to gather its bones and tell them her heart's desires. The girl told the carp's bones that all she wanted was a proper dress to attend the spring festival. Immediately her rags turned into a silk gown with golden slippers. Yeh-Shen was the most beautiful girl at the festival, but she had to run home to avoid her stepmother, and she lost a slipper along the way. A merchant found her slipper and brought it to the king, who swore he must marry the owner of such a perfect shoe. Of all the women in the entire kingdom, Yeh-Shen was the only one who could wear the slipper. She married the king, and of course, they lived happily ever after.

Seal

Stories about the seal abound among folk living along the ocean's edge. Many believe that these sleek sea mammals are the source of tales about the mermaid, the seductive creature that is half human and half fish. These beliefs may have originated because when viewed from a distance, a seal basking on the rocks or with its head bobbing above the waves can look almost human.

The Inuit of Greenland and Northern Canada often depicted Sedna, the all-powerful goddess of the sea and source of all sea life, as a seal. When Sedna sent one of her seals to the Inuit, they were careful not to waste the precious gift. They ate the seal meat, made their homes and clothes of sealskin, and used seal bone for tools and weapons. Whenever a hunter captured a seal he would thank it for giving its life that his people might live.

Some families living on the Orkney and Shetland Islands in the North Sea between Ireland and Scotland claim to be descended from shape-shifting seals called *selkies*. Legend says that long ago a young fisherman saw a selkie shed her sealskin and transform into a lovely girl. Dazzled by her beauty, he stole the selkie's sealskin as she danced on the shore, trapping her in her human form. The fisherman married the selkie that very day. Each year on their anniversary, the selkie wife begged the fisherman to return her skin, and each year he refused. When the couple had been married ten years, the husband decided the selkie had been a wife and mother so long that she would have no desire to return to the sea, so he gave her the sealskin when she asked for it. But the call of the sea was too strong for her to resist: with a gasp of joy, the selkie wife ran to the shore, drew the skin around her, and dove into the ocean, a seal forevermore.

Frog

Wherever there are freshwater ponds and rivers, the husky croaking of frogs can be heard. Not surprisingly, these shy amphibians are a potent symbol of the force of water in cultures everywhere.

An Australian Aboriginal creation myth tells of a great frog who drank all the water in the world. The other animals suffered terribly from the resulting drought and decided that their only hope for survival was to make frog laugh hard enough to spit up the water. Eel was the one to succeed. The Huron Indians of North America tell a similar story, but in this version the creation god, Ioskeha, punctured the greedy frog like a water balloon.

Perhaps because they are often more visible after a storm, frogs are also associated with rain and fertility. Hindu folklore maintains that the frog brings rain when it croaks and that pouring water over a frog can break a drought. The ancient Egyptians depicted Heqit, the goddess of childbirth, with the head of a frog, and they used a frog or tadpole to symbolize pregnancy.

In Europe the best known frog story is a fairy tale. Once upon a time, a young princess tossed her golden ball into a deep pool. The princess cried so bitterly at the loss of her favorite toy that a frog heard her sobs. He offered to retrieve the golden ball if the princess would share her plate with him at dinner, let him sleep on her pillow, and wake him the next morning with a kiss. Eager to have her toy back, the princess agreed, but once the ball was back in her hand, she ran off home. That night, however, the frog appeared at the castle to demand she honor her word. Ashamed of her behavior, the princess shared her plate with the frog at dinner and let him sleep on her pillow. In the morning she woke him with a kiss, which was the magical solution to a magical problem: the frog was an enchanted prince who needed the love of a princess to transform back into a man. No longer a frog, the prince offered to make the princess his bride, and she happily agreed.

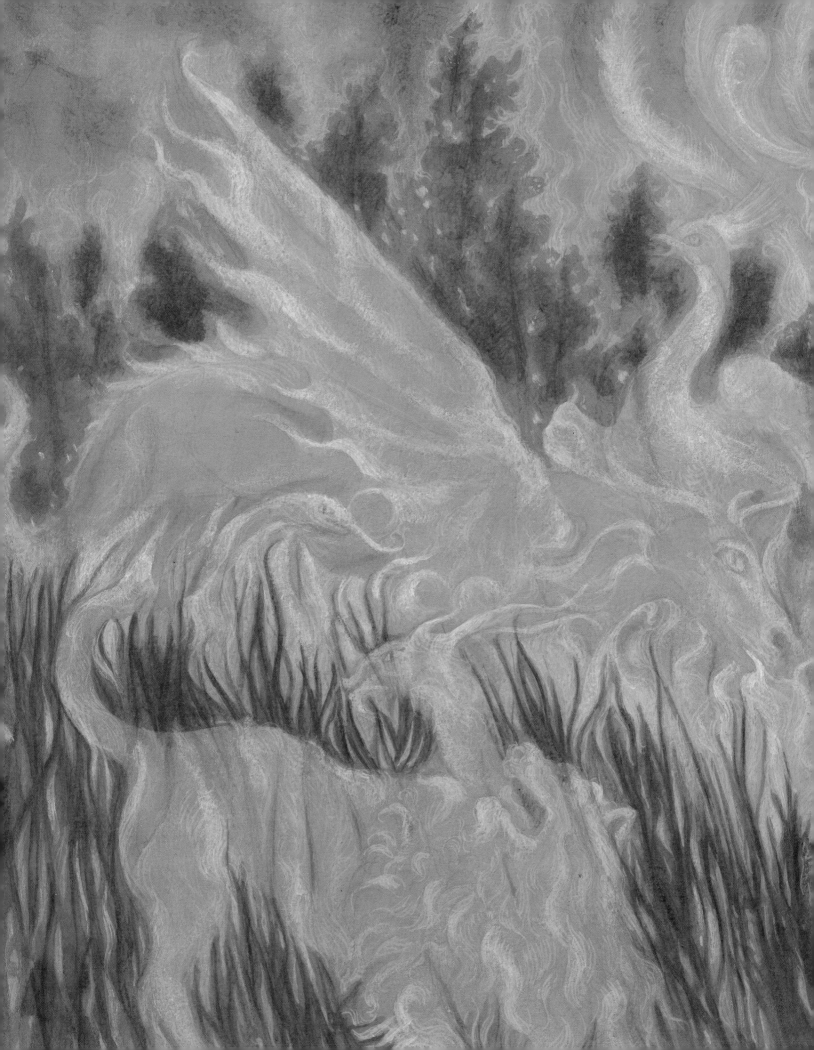

FIRE

Falcon

Dragon

Chimera

Phoenix

Falcon

(HAWK)

Soaring high above the earth, the falcon truly looks as if it could fly to the sun. No wonder these golden-eyed hawks have long been associated with sunlight as they shoot directly to their destination like a tongue of flame. Loki, the roguish Norse god of fire, was said to take the form of a falcon when he wanted to eavesdrop on his fellow gods or to escape quickly the scene of his latest mischief. Hawks were also favorite birds of the Greco-Roman sun god, Apollo.

Falcons have long been a symbol of royalty. At one time in most parts of Europe, only those with royal blood were allowed to hunt with peregrine falcons, the largest of these regal hawks. Lesser nobles were allowed to hunt with smaller falcons, but the common folk were barred from the sport of falconry altogether. A royal hawk figures prominently in Hungarian mythology as well. The divine falcon, Turul, impregnated the legendary queen, Emese, in a dream. When her baby was born, a stream of molten fire poured from the queen's breast, signaling the birth of Almos, the hero who would found Hungary.

In ancient Egypt the god Horus was depicted either as a falcon or a falcon-headed man. Just as the pharaoh reigned supreme over the land, Horus ruled over the sun and sky. He was the son of Isis, the fertility goddess, and Osiris, lord of the afterlife. The falcon, as his symbol, was revered by the Egyptians. These hawks were allowed to prey on domestic pigeons and ducks without fear of reprisal—no one would dream of risking the wrath of Horus by harming the national bird. Nor was any public festivity celebrated without first asking Horus's blessing. Falcons were raised in his temples to take part in these ceremonies. Ancient records suggest that people made rich donations for the priests to also bring a temple falcon to private functions, such as the signing of marriage and business contracts. They believed that the presence of the sacred bird would ensure success.

Dragon

Dragons are among the most magical mythical creatures of the world. In the Far East, dragons are regarded as protective forces associated with water, but in the western world they are creatures of fire. While our modern image of the fire-breathing dragon has its roots mostly in Nordic and Celtic myths, Greek legend was also rich in dragon stories. Perhaps the most famous dragon from Greek mythology was Draco, which means "watcher" in Greek. Draco guarded the garden of the Hesperides for Hera, queen of the gods, and gave his life defending it. In honor of his service, Hera set him among the stars as a constellation.

Though they usually guarded treasure for themselves, dragons were also often cast as the keepers of golden hoards throughout Europe. These greedy creatures were winged lizards with flaming breath and a taste for human flesh. Their blood reputedly had magical powers. German myth tells of the dragon Fafnir, whose lair on the banks of the Rhine included an enchanted helmet that could make the wearer disappear. Fafnir was finally slain by the hero Siegfried, who not only won the helmet of invisibility but also gained the ability to understand the language of birds from a taste of the dragon's blood.

In the British Isles, the dragon is best remembered as the legendary foe of a warrior saint. Saint George was a soldier who lived in Asia Minor during the fourth century, but England claimed his legend for its own during the Middle Ages. The poet Edmund Spenser transformed the saint into the Red Cross Knight, a noble English youth raised by fairies and sent by their queen to do brave deeds in her name. George's first task was to slay a dragon that was menacing a far kingdom. The untried knight battled the dragon an entire day, and by nightfall he was at the end of his strength. But as George slept, a magical spring bubbled up around him to bathe his wounds. When he awoke the next morning, the young hero was healed and able to vanquish the dragon. George continued to fight evil in service to the Faerie Queen, earning his place as national hero and patron saint of England.

Chimera

Chimera—pronounced Ki-MIR-uh—was as frightful as she was fantastic. Described by the Greek epic poet Homer in the ninth century B.C.E. as part lion, part serpent, and part goat, this fearsome creature breathed noxious flames and destroyed everything in her path. In Greek mythology Chimera was the daughter of Echidna, a giant serpent with the head of a beautiful nymph, and her loathesome hundred-headed mate, Typhon. Zeus killed the evil Typhon but spared Echidna and her horrible offspring, including Chimera, the three-headed dog Cerberus, and the Sphinx, so they might test the mettle of future heroes.

Chimera finally met her match in the hero Bellerophon, although he did have divine help. The night before he was to face the monster, Minerva, the goddess of wisdom, appeared to him in a dream holding a golden bridle. She told him that in the morning he would find the winged horse, Pegasus, waiting at a nearby spring to carry him into battle, and if he followed her advice, he could defeat Chimera. Bellerophon awoke with the bridle in his hand and found Pegasus just where the goddess said he would. Then, mounted on his magical steed, he flew off to face Chimera. Following Minerva's instructions, Bellerophon tipped his spear with a lump of lead. When he thrust the weapon down Chimera's hot throat, the lead melted inside her, causing instant death.

In the Greek language, the word *chimera* means "she-goat," but today it has come to describe any extraordinary creature bearing the parts of many animals. These monsters appear in stories around the world. Mesopotamian myth told of benign genies with the heads and wings of eagles, but the bodies of men who acted as messengers between gods and mortals. The ancient Zapotec people of Oaxaca, Mexico, believed that amazing crossbred animals visited people in their dreams, bringing spiritual messages and advice from the spirit plane. To this day Zapotec artisans create beautifully painted copal wood carvings of these dream animals, which are called *alebrijes*.

Phoenix

The phoenix is a universal symbol for immortality. The legend of a great bird that dies and is reborn in fire has roots in many cultures through the ages. Perhaps the oldest of these marvelous creatures is the Chinese phoenix, called the *feng-huang*, which has figured prominently in folklore for over seven thousand years as the embodiment of harmony and perfect grace. The feng-huang's song was supposed to be exceptionally beautiful and include all five notes of the classical Chinese musical scale. Its brilliant plumage included all five basic colors. Its body was composed of the six celestial spheres, and in its bill it carried the scrolls of sacred knowledge. This bird appeared only to herald a remarkable event or good fortune before disappearing indefinitely. For centuries the feng-huang was also the Chinese imperial symbol of the empress.

Another ancient myth tells of the *benu*, an Egyptian sun bird associated with the sun god, Re, and Osiris, the resurrected god of the afterlife. The benu was often depicted as a heron with fabulous red and gold plumage. A symbol of renewal, the benu was said to rise each morning from an eternal flame that burned atop a sacred persea tree in Heliopolis, the city of the sun, and to return to the tree to be consumed by the flame each evening at sunset.

The Greeks incorporated elements of the benu story into their own myth of the phoenix, a fabulous bird that lived deep in the Arabian desert. They believed only one phoenix existed, and that every five hundred years it would build a nest of rare spices and aromatic woods that would be set aflame by the sun. As it settled upon this pyre, the phoenix sang a song of surpassing sweetness that drew all the birds of the world to witness its death. But though the flames consumed the bird, it was not destroyed. Instead, it was reborn from the flames to live for another five hundred years, thus continuing the eternal cycle of life and death.

SELECTED SOURCES

Ann, Martha, and Dorthy Myers Imel. *Goddesses in World Mythology*. Oxford, New York, Toronto: Oxford University Press, 1993.

Bulfinch, Thomas. *Bulfinch's Mythology*. New York: Signet/New American Library, 1962.

Carlyon, Richard. *A Guide to the Gods: An Essential Guide to World Mythology*. New York: William Morrow, 1981.

Cavendish, Richard. *Mythology: An Illustrated Encyclopedia*. Boston: Little, Brown, 1992.

Cooper, J. C. *An Illustrated Encyclopaedia of Traditional Symbols*. London: Thames and Hudson, 1978.

Cotterel, Arthur. *The Macmillan Illustrated Encyclopedia of Myths and Legends*. New York: Macmillan, 1989.

Encyclopedia of World Mythology. Foreword by Rex Warner. New York: Galahad Books, 1975.

Fitzhugh, William W., and Aron Crowell. *Crossroads of Continents: Cultures of Siberia and Alaska*. Washington, D.C.: Smithsonian Institution Press, 1988.

Grimal, Pierre, ed. *Larousse World Mythology*. London: Hamlyn Publishing Group, 1968.

Philip, Neil. *The Illustrated Book of Myths: Tales and Legends of the World*. New York and London: Dorling Kindersley, 1995.

Piggott, Juliet. *Japanese Mythology*. London: Peter Bedrick Books, 1982.

Sproul, Barbara C. *Primal Myths: Creation Myths Around the World*. New York: Harper San Francisco, 1979.

Walker, Barbara G. *The Woman's Encyclopedia of Myths and Secrets*. New York: Harper San Francisco, 1983.

Willis, Roy, gen. ed. *World Mythology*. New York: Henry Holt, 1993.